DI028262

THUCYDIDES
THE SPEECHES OF PERICLES

MILESTONES OF THOUGHT

THUCYDIDES

THE SPEECHES OF PERICLES

*Translated with an Introduction,
Notes, and Comments by*

H. G. Edinger

FREDERICK UNGAR PUBLISHING CO.

New York

MILESTONES OF THOUGHT
in the History of Ideas

Library of Congress Catalog Card Number 78-4304
ISBN 0-8044-6908-3

CONTENTS

CHRONOLOGY

(All dates are B.C.)

490   The Greeks led by Athens repulse the Persian invasion at Marathon.

?490   Birth of Pericles.

480   Greeks repulse a second Persian invasion at the sea battle of Salamis.

479   Greeks defeat the Persian army at the land battle of Plataea.

478   Athens leads in the formation of the Delian League, an alliance against Persia.

472   Pericles serves as producer of Aeschylus' *Persians*.

461   Beginning of Pericles' political prominence.

?460   Birth of Thucydides.

456   Death of Aeschylus, playwright born 525.

454   Treasury of the Delian League moved from the island of Delos to Athens.

449   Formal peace arranged with Persia.

446   Thirty Years' Peace arranged between Athens and Sparta.

443   Beginning of Pericles' political ascendancy.

438   Phidias' gold and ivory statue of Athena dedicated on the Acropolis.

NOTE

Numbers within parentheses in the text and in the running heads indicate Book, chapter, and section of Thucydides' original Greek works. Thus 1.141.2 refers to Book 1, chapter 141, section 2.

INTRODUCTION

❧❦❧

I. THE AGE OF PERICLES

When Pericles delivered his Funeral Speech, with its praise of Athenian civilization, a veritable galaxy of outstanding men were alive and working in the city of Athens. They included the tragedians Sophocles, Euripides, and Aristophanes; Socrates, the philosopher; Phidias, the sculptor; and Ictinus, the architect of the Parthenon. Thucydides, the historian, was a young man already contemplating the writing of his illustrious *History*. In addition to these sublime names, there was a large number of lesser writers and artists, particularly minor masters of pottery and painting, as well as prominent military and political figures like Nicias, Demosthenes, Alcibiades, and Pericles himself. Eminent foreign figures, like Herodotus, Gorgias, and Protagoras, had visited or would visit Athens, attracted by its position of leadership in the Greek world. There never lived so many great cultural figures in one city and at one time. Athens in the Age of Pericles was a city overflowing with unsurpassed creative energy.

Pericles, in the last of the speeches translated here,

1

said that when the Athenian empire went into decline, men would look back upon it as unique. But his reason for its uniqueness was not the abundance of creative energy in the empire, but the fact that Athenians "as Greeks extended their rule over more other Greeks than anyone else." Pericles' perspective was military, because his speeches, as we know them from Thucydides, were delivered either in wartime or shortly before the war broke out. They were addressed to wartime questions, not to evaluations of Athenian cultural achievements. Furthermore, they were recorded by a historian whose main interest was to study the growth and use of power for military objectives.

The perspective of modern students and admirers of the Age of Pericles is very likely to be cultural in the more narrow sense, springing as it might from an interest in the art of this age. Pericles' military perspective and his cultural view of Athens do not, however, exclude each other, and the area in which they overlap is by no means small. Pericles refers to the cultural attractions of Athens not, as we shall see, just in passing, but as an important factor in his praise about Athenian greatness. Today's admirer of ancient Athens should realize from Pericles' arguments that there is a close relationship between the vigor of Athenian culture and the scope and aggressiveness of its imperial enterprise under a democratic form of government.

Beyond this partial agreement of two views of the Golden Age of Athens is a more basic relationship. Crucial to the modern admiration of that age is the unity that its arts possess, a unity of style and expression, a mature self-sufficiency. Crucial, also, is the idea that the thought, poetry, sculpture, and architecture of this circumscribed, perhaps parochial, but vigorous culture should possess qualities that have been admired for centuries far beyond their time and place.

Pericles, in his speeches in Thucydides' *History*, draws an inspiring picture of Athenian unity and vigor, but only in the sphere of government and military activity. If only his First and Third Speeches were recorded by Thucydides, this emphasis on unity would appear to be merely the call to submerge differences and pull together in the face of the enemy, a call that any statesman must make in time of war. But, in the Funeral Speech, the unity of will and resolution necessary for wartime is explained on far deeper levels, and the call to unity is expanded into an idealized picture of an Athens that has already attained the conditions of enduring eminence.

II. THUCYDIDES AND PERICLES

In the spring of 431 B.C., an army led by Spartans from the south of Greece moved northward and eastward to invade the territory known as Attica, of which the largest city was Athens. This invasion was the beginning of a war that was to be fought, off and on, for twenty-seven years. About the time fighting started, or somewhat earlier, Thucydides began to gather material for a history of the war. He continued to collect information and to work on his book all during the war, but when he died, some four or five years after its end, his book was left unfinished. It breaks off in the course of narrating the events of the twenty-first year of the war. Because the Spartans were at the head of a league of Greek cities, many of which were located in the southern part of Greece called the Peloponnese, the war is known as the Peloponnesian War.

Thucydides' *History* is thus specifically a history of the conflict between Sparta and Athens from 431–404 B.C., which Thucydides regards as one war, although it was interrupted by a long truce. His chief reasons for beginning the *History* were not only the stature of the two warring cities, Sparta and Athens, which were then at the peak of their power, but also the large number of allies on each side. Thucydides concentrates on the military course of the war; while economic, political, and cultural questions are dealt with in a subordinate way. Thucydides' *History* is therefore not what we moderns would call a *History of Greece*. Given these limitations, however, Thucydides, convinced of the greatness of his subject and bringing to his task an acute understanding of the stakes of the conflict, gave a powerful and profoundly moving analysis.

Thucydides, as an Athenian, tells the story largely from the point of view of Athens. His own position during the war was unusual. He had been elected, probably in his mid-thirties, by the Athenian Assembly to the board of ten generals (the *stragegia*) in 424 B.C. The election would indicate a reasonably high standing and prominence within Athenian society. As a member of the staff of generals, Thucydides would undertake command of Athenian land and sea forces as required during his year in office. He was doing this in the autumn of 424, in the northern Aegean near Thrace. The major action in the region at this time was the siege by Athenians of a town called Amphipolis. Thucydides' naval detachment became involved in this campaign, and he was called upon to arrive at Amphipolis with reinforcements. His detachment failed to arrive on time, and Amphipolis was lost. This military blunder forced Thucydides to go into exile. He was barred from returning to Athens or its territories during the course of the war. Where he stayed or traveled during his exile is not known. He was, however, able to obtain information from both sides for use in the *History*. From the point of view of a writer, his position was uniquely advantageous. He was a general, although disgraced, and he was free of duties; he could consult with those who were familiar with both sides of the war. The *History*, therefore, though written largely from the Athenian point of view, has a vision of the war that is probably far more balanced than it would have been had Thucydides spent the war in Athens in the service of his native city.

Thucydides grew up during the ascendancy of Pericles, and most students of the *History* recognize that there is a crucial relationship underlying Pericles' rise to power and Thucydides' writing of the *History*. Nowhere in the *History* does Thucydides offer a summary of the stages by which Pericles came to dominate Athenian political life. The place for such a summary might have been in the first book, just before the First Speech of Pericles is quoted, but Thucydides did not find it suitable to include such material. We do know that Pericles descended from a prominent and aristocratic family and that he was involved throughout his career with strengthening the democracy of Athens and with maintaining the empire. From about 461 B.C., he held one of the ten prestigious positions on the *strategia* almost every year until his death. The generals were elected year to year and they were accountable to the Assembly. Another source of Pericles' eminence should therefore be found in his ability as a speaker in the Assembly, which meant his ability to conceive, explain, and defend policies that the Assembly might be persuaded to adopt as the policy of Athens. And so, Thucydides represents him as urging the Athenians to accept the inevitable war with Sparta in 432, and also as having a grand strategy for winning the war. Not only was he able to persuade the Athenians to accept war and a strategy that he persuaded them to adopt; what is more, he checked their overenthusiasm or buoyed their fallen spirits; all this was accomplished through the sheer force of his oratory.

The question of war with Sparta is closely linked to

the history of the Athenian empire. After the retreat of the Persian land armies in 479 B.C., Athens led in the formation of a defensive alliance called the Delian League. The purpose of this League was to oppose further activities of Persia in the Aegean area. But Persia's defeat and the subsequent emergence of the League led to a rapid expansion of Athenian power, of her naval strength in particular; it had been crucial in the wars with Persia and was now carefully maintained. Pericles' rise to prominence, beginning about 461, was linked to a very aggressive phase of Athenian expansion. The resistance to Persia required sometimes distant and elaborate military expeditions, and these in turn required the maintenance and expansion of the fleet, as well as the close control of the allies in the League. There were frictions and disputes within the League in addition to Athens's rivalry with other large cities, first with Corinth, then with Sparta. When the joint treasury of the League was moved from the island of Delos to the Acropolis of Athens, the predominance of Athens over her allies was clearly established. Not only was this continued growth of Athenian power achieved under Pericles' leadership, but also the expansion of Athens's democratic institutions became unmistakably evident. The Athenian empire had come of age.

The League supported Athens financially, and consequently, there were always an expansionist tendency in the Assembly's policies. But one of the cardinal points of the strategy that Pericles always emphasized in his speeches was the necessity to avoid the acquisition of new imperial territory. Yet, in the Funeral Speech, he also makes clear that Athens enjoys a large number of advantages unique in Greece because of her control of an empire. And, as we have noted, it is this broad power base that Pericles expected to be the foundation of Athens's future glory.

III.   THE SPEECHES IN THUCYDIDES

A remarkable feature of the *History* is the large number of speeches that are quoted in it. This reflects both the importance of oratory in ancient society and Thucydides' intentions as a historian. He might well have chosen to include fewer speeches or none, but found it very useful to do otherwise. Among these speeches, the Funeral Speech, whose significance I have already noted, is often read and studied separately from the rest of the *History*. Two other speeches of Pericles are also included here, as well as a fairly long summary of a fourth. Although the Funeral Speech is regarded as a work of unique effectiveness, it is perhaps more instructive to read all the speeches of Pericles together, for together they provide a good introduction to many aspects of Thucydides' presentation of the war.

The delivery of public orations was not an occasional, or strictly ceremonial, practice in Athens or in any phase of classical civilization. It was the chief means by which a leader could communicate with the people. In the democracy of Athens, where decisions were made after public debate in the Assembly, oratory was an essential skill of a political leader. Also, the law courts were so constituted that oratory played a large role there, and there were many public occasions at which an orator of ability was required. Rhetoric was a main subject of higher education, and there were famous schools and teachers devoted to it. It also appears as an element in epic poetry, and in tragic and comic drama.

The importance of public speaking in Athens becomes clearer from a brief review of the organization of the government. The main decision-making power in the city was vested in the Assembly, a body made up of all eligible citizens. The Assembly (or *ekklesía*) met at least forty times a year. Its purpose was to debate and vote on proposals brought forward for its consideration by a committee of its members, called the boulé. The offices of the government were held by citizens elected annually. The only exception to this yearly change of office-holders was the military office of *strategós*. Ten *strategoí* were chosen each year to supervise the activities of the army and fleet; a *strategós* could succeed himself in the office. The law courts were essentially committees of the Assembly. Jurors were chosen by lot, and the decisions of the jury were by majority vote and final. As to the size of the membership in the Assembly, boulé, and juries: Every full Athenian male citizen was entitled to attend the Assembly; he might be chosen by lot to become a member of the boulé or jury. The size of the attendance at the Assembly varied; the average attendance could be as high as 6,000. The boulé, the body that formulated motions for debate, had a fixed membership of 500. Juries varied in size from 200 to 1,000.

The Assembly was the final voice on all matters of state. Not all meetings were heavily attended. But on such a question as whether or not to reject an ultimatum from Sparta in 432, the interest and attendance were high. Practice and skill in the art of oratory were necessary to present ideas before a large meeting and to persuade the voters to choose your course of action over that of other men. The leading figures of Athenian public life had many opportunities to acquire that practice and to develop that skill. In fact, Thucydides and many other Athenian writers give the impression that no man of prominence in the city lacked the ability to compose and deliver a spirited, and persuasive speech.

Thucydides' decision to include a great number of speeches in his *History* therefore reflects an important aspect of Athenian public life. How these speeches reflect the purposes of the historian is a more complicated question. Clearly, Thucydides was writing about widely scattered events over a long period of time. Most likely he had first-hand knowledge of many important speeches and reliable reports of others. But it is not likely that he knew the authentic text of all the speeches that he reports. The problem is raised by Thucydides himself early in the *History*.

> As for the speeches in this history, some were delivered before the war broke out, others while it was in progress. I heard some of them myself, while I learned about others from various sources. In all cases it was difficult to remember them word for word, so my practice in writing has been to give the speakers the words that I thought would have been demanded of them by the circumstances, while keeping as closely as possible to the arguments they actually used.

This statement raises various questions, which could be answered only if a selection of the speeches in verbatim transcript were available so that they could be compared with Thucydides' versions. Thucydides clearly does not present any of the speeches as transcripts. Aside from his own statement above, there is the clear fact that many of the speeches are much shorter than could be expected. Thucydides has also been very selective in choosing the speeches that he quotes or summarizes. Lastly, he has not made any appreciable attempt to characterize the speakers by their personal style; the literary style of all the speeches is largely uniform and it is convincingly his own.

Granted that the speeches are not documentary, that they are compressed and introduced very selectively, the question remains why Thucydides wanted to include them at all. As a partial explanation, it can be said that the *History* is built around the interplay between the speeches and the narrative. Speakers debate the wisdom or folly of a particular course of action. In the narrative, the action taken and its consequences are revealed. In

general, the speeches are abstract and analytical, calcu-
lated to appeal to the individual reader more than to an
entire assembly or army. Thucydides often presents pairs
or sets of speeches, one for each side of a debate, not so
much for historical realism as for clarity in the delinea-
tion of issues as he sees them. By this device, the reader
can grasp the motivations of two opposing groups or
speakers. Therefore, while the speeches represent the
abstract, analytical portion of the writing, the narrative
is an account of what actually happened.

Added to the problem of determining the historian's
criteria of content and purpose in the speeches is that of
the actual writing of the *History*. Thucydides says that
he began work on his book as soon as the war broke out.
But scholars rightly distinguish between the gathering
and note-taking that would mark the beginning of work
and the actual writing of the *History*. It is precarious to
decide this long-debated question, but it is safe to say
that a very large body of recent Thucydidean scholarship
holds that the largest part of the *History* in its final form
was done by Thucydides only after the war had ended.
That he was writing with the advantage of hindsight is
obvious in many places. That is, when he wrote the first
two books in their final form, most of the war, if not all,
had passed, so that he could form a definite judgment of
the place that Pericles and his policies should have in the
History. The three speeches in which Pericles expounds
on his policy and his understanding of Athenian life are
selected here, and their arguments are reproduced, for
reasons that Thucydides would not have known at the
time that the speeches were delivered.

Thucydides composed the speeches in his own style
following the practice of all ancient historians, but it
must not be forgotten, however, that the arguments of
the speeches are those of the speakers.

No original political speeches from Athens of the

time of Pericles survive except for very few fragmentary phrases. He was famous particularly for his striking use of metaphor. Examples of these figures of speech are recorded by various commentators. But such minute scraps do not permit a judgment of the actual nature of Pericles' oratory. His great reputation as a powerful speaker, current in antiquity and confirmed by the eye-witness judgment of Thucydides, rests on speeches whose originals are now lost. The versions of Thucydides are nevertheless a precious record of the living Pericles. The force of his words in the *History* derives from his well-constructed arguments, his nobility of attitude, the detached seriousness of his approach, and from the moving conception of Athens and its history. Thucydides does not indicate his own judgment of these speeches in comparison to others, but he does record that both the First and Third Speeches fully achieved their objectives, to persuade the people of Pericles' point of view. The Funeral Speech has taken on a force of its own, impressing modern readers with the unequalled grandeur of Athens in the Age of Pericles.

THE FIRST SPEECH

❧

(140) My views are the same as ever: we must not make any concession to the Spartans, although I know that the enthusiasm of people when they enter upon a war is not retained when it comes to action, and that their mood is altered by the course of events.

But I see that today I must give you the same or almost the same advice, as I have given you in the past. Those who are persuaded by my arguments must faithfully support the decision that we reach together, even if every single event does not turn out in our favor, as is likely to happen. Either support the decision now or you will not be able to claim any credit, after we win the war, for having acted wisely. Everyone knows, of course, that events in war do not turn out any more predictably than any other plans that people make. And when something happens contrary to expectations, people talk about it in terms of their good luck or bad luck.

The Spartans have plotted against us in the past, and now most intensely. The treaty[1] provided that each side mutually bring its differences to arbitration, and that, pending arbitration, each side keep what it has. But they have never offered arbitration, nor accepted from us any such offer. They want to have their complaints settled by war, not by negotiation, and they are here not simply to lodge a protest but to deliver an ultimatum. Specifically they are ordering us to lift the siege of Potidaea,[2] to give Aigina[3] her independence, and to revoke the Megarian Decree.[4] And finally they have come here to proclaim boldly that we must give freedom to all Greeks everywhere.

They offer a special assurance that if we revoke the Megarian Decree there will be no war. Now let none of you think that the war that would come if we refuse would be a war about some small matter. You must not have any lingering thought that you have gone to war about some trifle. In fact the Megarian Decree is the supreme test of your resoluteness; it will prove whether your policy is correct. If you yield to the Spartans on this point, they will immediately make another, greater demand, because they will believe that you made your concession because you were afraid. But if you take a strong stand on this point, you will make absolutely clear that they must treat you as equals.

(141) But you must make your decision. You must decide between the alternatives. You can yield to their demands and avoid suffering immediate harm. Or we can go to war, as I think we should, and whether the war comes over an important or trivial matter, it will still be clear that we do not intend to give in and that we are going to keep what we have without showing any fear. When one power makes demands of another equal power about important or trivial matters, and when it makes no offer to negotiate them, then it would be only slaves who would yield to them.

Listen attentively to the state of preparation and the resources of each side, for I want you to realize clearly that ours is not the weaker position. For one thing, the Spartans can depend only on their own resources; they

do not have surplus wealth, either private or public.
They also have no experience of prolonged wars or of
naval warfare. Their expeditions against others only last
a short time, because of their poverty. Thus they cannot
send out well-equipped fleets or even land-armies very
often, since that means absence from their own land and
having to pay expenses out of their private funds. Besides that, we have effective control of the sea. To sustain
military campaigns, available reserves are always more
effective than emergency taxes. The Spartans, having to
farm their own land, worry more about their property
than their lives. They believe they will survive safe and
sound, but they are not so sure that their property will
not all be gone, especially if a war proves to be lengthy.[5]
Although they do not expect it, that is quite likely to
happen.

Now, in a single battle, the Peloponnesians and
their allies could stand up against all the other Greeks,
but they do not have the ability to sustain a war against
an adversary who has resources so different from their
own. And one resource they lack is the ability to make
quick decisions in emergencies. They cannot do this because they do not have a central body for making decisions. As a result, each Spartan ally is concerned for his
own individual interests. There is no power among them
that can outweigh all the others when it comes to a vote,
and they are not even all of the same racial background.
No decisive actions can ever result from those conditions.
Some of the Spartan allies are trying as hard as possible
to avenge another ally, while others want only to insure
that their own territories suffer the least possible damage. Sparta and her allies confer only at long intervals
and then they use only a fraction of their time to consider their common interests. Most of their time is spent
in arranging their own private concerns. It does not
occur to any of them that the whole alliance will suffer

because of one ally's lack of interest. Instead, each state thinks that some other member will consider it his responsibility. As a result, their whole common policy is weakened and this fact remains unperceived, although they think that they agreed upon a common course of action.

(142) The main point, however, is this: because of the lack of liquid funds they will attempt to raise, and because of the delay involved, their war effort will suffer. In war, opportunity waits for no man.

You don't have to be afraid of their naval preparations or of their attempt to build fortifications in Attica. Even in peacetime, it is difficult to build fortifications as large as a town. Any attempt of theirs will take place during wartime and, more importantly, when we already have fortifications to stand up to them. If they merely establish some minor outpost, they might do some damage by raiding and also by receiving deserters, but the base would never be strong enough to prevent us from using our fleet and from establishing bases in their territory while we protect ourselves with our fleet, which is the strongest part of our power.

We have, in fact, more power on land than they do because of our experience at sea, while their experience in land warfare gives them no advantage at sea. And it will not be easy for them to acquire enough naval experience to become experts. Even you, who have been practicing the art of naval operations ever since the Persian invasions, have not become perfect masters of it. How then could their soldiers ever presume to make much progress? They are farmers, not sailors, and even beyond that, they are effectively prevented from gaining any experience by systematically being blockaded by our large fleet. Against a blockage of only a few ships they might be encouraged to dismiss their lack of skill and risk a battle because of the numbers of their boats. But

when, in fact, they are pressed by a large number of
boats, they will not take the offensive; they will become
less and less skillful because they are not getting the
experience. And as a result, they will become more and
more cautious. Effective seamanship is only learned by
practice, like any other skill. You can't engage in seamanship like in a hobby, to be picked up in one's spare
time. On the contrary, maintaining a high standard of
seamanship does not leave spare time for anything else.

(143) Suppose the Spartans attempt to appropriate
the treasures[6] at Delphi or at Olympia, and, by offering
higher rates of pay than they could otherwise afford, do
better than Athens in hiring foreign sailors. This would
be a serious situation if we did not outnumber them in
terms of citizens and resident aliens who can serve as
marines. But we do outnumber them in that respect, and
there is a far more impressive fact: we have citizens who
can serve as helmsmen and as crew members, and we
have more of them and better trained ones than all the
rest of Greece put together. Also, if it comes to an actual
battle, none of the foreigners they might hire would
think of becoming an exile from his homeland and of
fighting along with the Spartans for a few days' extra
pay, no matter how large a windfall it might be, when
the chance of the Spartans' winning is so small.

As far as I can see, that is more or less the position of
the Spartans. And I believe that our own position does
not have in it the kinds of weaknesses that I described in
theirs. I believe, in fact, that it has advantages that
strongly outweigh theirs. If, for example, they attack our
territory by land, we shall be able to make a naval ex-
pedition against theirs. Even if they devastated all of
Attica, it would turn out that the devastation of a part of
the Peloponnese would be worse for them by comparison.
The Spartans would not be able to gain control of any
territory without fighting a battle on land, while we

would have plenty of land on the islands as well as on the mainland. In other words, our domination of the sea will be decisive. Look at it this way, if Athens were an island, who would be more invincible than we Athenians? As things are, we must adopt this 'island way of thinking' and be prepared to give up Attica and our farms, and safeguard the sea and the city. We must not join battle with Sparta out of anger over the loss of land and homes, for the Spartans are far more numerous than us. If we won such a battle, we should have to fight them again, and they would not be less numerous. If we were defeated, there would be additional defections of our allies, who are our strength. Athens' forces are not large enough to campaign against our allies if they all revolt. Above all, we should not lament the loss of farms and land, but only the loss of life. It is not homes and territories that produce men, but humans who control and use those things. And if I thought that I could persuade you, I would urge you to abandon your farms and territory, to destroy them, in fact, and thus demonstrate to the Spartans that you will not give in to them on account of those things.

(144) There are many other reasons for my belief that you should feel confident in ultimate victory. But one condition must be that you constantly reject any proposals to add to the empire during the war, and that you steadily resist the temptation to undertake risks that you can avoid. What I fear more than the strategies of our enemies is our own mistakes.

But I shall deal with all the details of planning on other occasions, when the discussions can be tied to the events of the war. For the present, I urge that you send the emissaries back to Sparta with these answers: if the Spartans stop applying their decree of expulsion of aliens to us and our allies, then we will allow the Megarians access to the markets and ports of the empire. (For in the

treaty there is no clause forbidding either those orders of
hers or our decree against Megara.) Furthermore, we
shall allow the various cities to choose their own government and be independent if they were independent
when we made the treaty, but we will do this only when
the Spartans, for their part, permit the cities of their
alliance to choose the form of government they wish, and
not the form suitable to Sparta. We should also answer
that we are willing to put our differences to arbitration
and that we will not be the side that starts the war, but
that we shall resist those who do start it. This is the right
reply, and this the reply that we should give.

It is essential for you to realize that the war is being
forced upon us, and the more determined we are to accept the challenge, the less eager will our enemies be to
attack us. We must also realize that, both for cities and
individuals, it is from the greatest danger that the greatest glory is won. Our forefathers did not have the resources that we have, yet they stood up against the Persian invaders and they even abandoned what they had.
It was by wisdom rather than by good luck, by courage
rather than by material power that they drove back the
barbarians. Their actions are the foundation of what our
city is today. We must not be less wise or less courageous
than they. We must resist the enemy in every way and
leave to our children a city as great as that we received
from our forefathers.

Notes to the First Speech

1. In 445 Athens and Sparta agreed to a treaty to settle
    their differences. This came to be known as the
    Thirty Years' Peace.
2. A town on the Chalcidian Peninsula in the northern
    Aegean which seceded from Athens in 433 and had
    been besieged by Athenian forces since 432.

3. Athens, by the terms of the Thirty Years' Peace, retained control over this large and important island in the Saronic Gulf.

4. This decree, proposed in the Assembly by Pericles, excluded the Megarians from using both the ports of the Athenian empire and Athenian Agora.

5. Pericles' prediction exemplifies his foresight. The first phase of the war lasted 10 years; the end of it did not come until 27 years after this speech.

6. The festival and religious centers at Delphi and Olympia had a group of treasury buildings which served as a kind of safe deposit vault. Various cities deposited large sums of money there for religious purposes.

Comments on the First Speech

Thucydides first records Pericles as a speaker at the very end of the first book of the *History*. Pericles had been a *strategós* many times before this occasion and had long been making contributions to the government of Athens. Thucydides does not refer to these earlier activities, but instead introduces Pericles as "the most eminent among Athenians of his time and the man of most ability both in debate and in action." Other Athenians voiced their views during the debate on the Megarian Decree, a fact duly noted, but only Pericles' speech is quoted and given in direct report. The reason for this is to add to the weight of Pericles' influence in the decision of the Assembly to accept war with Sparta, indeed to make it seem that Pericles alone persuaded the reluctant body of citizens to bring itself to resist Sparta.

We are shown Pericles, then, contributing to the debate in the Assembly, specifically giving advice on how best to reply to the proposals of a delegation that has arrived from Sparta. Thucydides says that this delegation brought an "ultimatum," so that the Athenian response would have to be decisive on the question of war or peace. Pericles recognizes that this is the case, says clearly that he expects war, and advises the Athenians to prepare for it. The alternative is "slavery" by surrender to Sparta. Acceptance of one demand, like the nullification of the Megarian Decree, would not bring peace, as the Spartans promise, but would only induce them to demand further concessions. Pericles argues that this is not an unworthy reason to go to war.

The Athenian public speaker must attempt to persuade the entire Assembly. Since Pericles has called for war, he must encourage the people to believe that war is a viable course of action for them. He therefore offers his analysis of the respective strengths and weaknesses of Sparta and Athens. This analysis, perhaps the heart of the speech, bears a relationship to both the Funeral Speech and the Third Speech. Like the Funeral Speech, it praises the Athenians and underscores the contrast between them and the Spartans. Like the Third Speech, it attempts to boost the self-confidence of the Athenians. The argument is based on the realities of money and manpower and also on Pericles' paradoxical analysis of the effect of sea power on the relative strengths of the two sides.

Pericles characterizes the Spartans above all as self-sufficient. They are land-based farmers without extensive contacts, either in war or peace, outside their own land. Whatever the historical reality at the time, the rhetorical effect is to make the Athenians think of the contrast between themselves and the Spartans. Pericles further emphasizes the contrast by recounting the way in which the Spartans and their allies make decisions. On this account, the Spartans lack the ability to make rapid decisions, they lack cohesion of purpose with their allies, and above all they lack a leader. They are, says Pericles, not even of the same "ancestral background." The contrast is with the Athenian empire, which, composed overwhelmingly of Ionian Greeks under Athenian leadership, extends through the Aegean and reflects the well-known liveliness and enterprising spirit of the Athenian character. If the Athenians know or believe these things about themselves and their allies, they will accept their favorable prospects for victory over Sparta in a war.

On the question of seamanship, Pericles speaks almost tauntingly about the Spartans. They cannot even hope to learn the art of seamanship, because Athens prevents them from getting the necessary practice. Again, the Spartan army is prevented by its location, having moved away from her land base, whereas Athens, controlling the sea, can exploit and control land anywhere she might choose, since her fleet can transport foot soldiers wherever necessary and protect them as they operate. Pericles, in a fine rhetorical stroke, asks the Athenians to imagine the happy security they would enjoy if Athens were an island, untouchable by land, invincible by sea. The fleets on each side must also be provided with manpower. Athens, says Pericles, has abundant skilled men and outranks Sparta in this respect, as is shown by Sparta's resort to mercenary sailors. But hiring mercenaries requires cash, which Sparta has been shown to lack. Pericles' arguments are made to seem convincing by being made so interdependent.

Pericles' call is for patriotism and self-confidence. Their land was handed down to them by their forefathers and must be handed down to those who will come after them. The Athenian way of life is so different that, almost more than anything else, it will defeat Sparta. In the Funeral Speech, Pericles will argue even more forcefully that Athens and the character of her citizens are unique. If Athenians understand their own uniqueness and if they understand how the military balance weighs in their favor, they will not lack confidence.

The rather abrupt opening of the speech is at first puzzling. Why should Pericles raise the question of his personal steadiness against the potential fickleness of the Assembly? The answer to this question goes to the heart of the problem of a leader in a direct democracy. The Assembly decides all policy. It is difficult to prevent the Assembly from yielding to the impulse of changing policy in pursuit of short-term gains. A responsible leader will persuade the Assembly to base its decisions on a long-term view. Hence, Pericles contrasts his personal constancy with the potential volatility of the Assembly. If it is difficult to decide on the right policy, it is even more difficult to maintain that policy. Pericles' warnings not to take advantage of fleeting opportunities for aggrandizement of the empire, and, in general, not to take unnecessary risks, are such essential tenets of his plan to win the war because he feared the inconstancy of the Assembly. He knows that they can easily be persuaded to snatch at a tempting gain or swagger into a losing risk. Athens as a city and Athenians as individuals can anticipate the rewards of victory only if they remain responsible and steady. He knows that only good leadership will achieve that stability.

SUMMARY
OF A SPEECH
⮜✦⮞

While the Spartans were still gathering at the Isthmus[1] and on their march there (before they invaded Attica), Pericles, son of Xanthippos, one of the ten generals,[2] realized that the invasion was coming. Because Archidamus happened to be a guest-friend[3] of his, Pericles became apprehensive that Archidamus, out of a personal desire to show his friendship for Pericles, might pass by his fields and not lay them waste.[4] He even feared that this might happen on orders from the Spartan leaders, as a means of discrediting him, in the same way that their ultimatum about "driving out the pollution"[5] had been aimed at him.

Pericles, therefore, spoke to the Athenians at a meeting of the Assembly saying that although Archidamus was his guest-friend, this fact would not result in any harm to Athens. With reference to his fields and buildings, he intended to give them up and make them public property, if the Spartans did not destroy them in the same way as those of other citizens. He did not want to incur the slightest suspicion on that account.

He went on to give his views about the current situation, and his advice was the same as before. The

Athenians should prepare carefully for war and bring their possessions from the country into Athens. They should not leave the city and battle outside it, but come inside the city and defend it. They should finish the fitting out of the fleet, in which their strength lay. They should, he said, maintain close control over their allies, and he pointed out the Athenian power derived from the allies in the form of payments of tribute. Wars, he said, were usually won by wise policy and a large reserve of money.

He told them to be heartened by the economic facts. There was an average of six hundred talents per year in tribute[6] coming to Athens from the allies, apart from their other usual income. They also had remaining at that time on the Acropolis six thousand talents in coined silver. (The maximum amount in this fund had been nine thousand ninety-seven hundred talents, from which expenditures had been made for the Propylaea[7] on the Acropolis and other building projects, and for the defense of Potidaia.[8]) In addition, Pericles mentioned the uncoined gold and silver that was on the Acropolis in the form of public and private dedications;[9] and all the equipment that was used in religious processions and festivals; all the booty from the Persian wars,[10] and other items of that kind. The total value of these objects was not less than five hundred talents. To these could be added the fairly large reserves of the other temples, which they could use, and if everything else was exhausted, they could use the sculptured gold attached to the statue of Athena.[11] He revealed that the statue had on it a weight of forty talents of refined gold, which was entirely removable. He said, however, that if they used this in an emergency, they would have to replace at least its full value.

This inventory that he made of their cash reserves encouraged them. As for hoplites[12] in the army, he said that there were thirteen thousand, not counting the ones stationed in outlying garrisons and in the city's defenses, who numbered sixteen thousand. (That was the number originally assigned to serve defensively wherever the enemy invaded. They came from the oldest and youngest age groups and included all the metics[13] who served as hoplites.)

As for defenses, there were 35 stadia of wall[14] running from the city to Phaleron, in addition to the perimeter wall of the city, of which the part kept guarded was 43 stadia. Part of the perimeter wall, the portion between the Long Walls and the walls to Phaleron, was not guarded. There were also the Long Walls running from Athens down to the Piraeus, which were 40 stadia long, and whose outer faces were guarded. The complete circuit of the wall around the Piraeus, including Munychia, was 60 stadia, of which half was kept under guard.

He mentioned 1,200 in the cavalry, including mounted archers; 1,600 archers on foot; and 300 triremes[15] equipped to sail immediately.

This was the state of Athens' military readiness when the Spartans were first about to invade. However, even Pericles underestimated the extent of Athens' military strength.

Pericles also added other arguments, as he usually did, to prove that Athens would be victorious in the war.

Notes to Summary of a Speech

1. The Isthmus is the narrow neck of land that joins the Peloponnesus to the northern and eastern parts of mainland Greece. The armies of Sparta and its allies assembled there as the point from which to invade Athenian territory.
2. The Athenian Assembly elected annually a group

of ten *strategoi* or generals to conduct the actions of the army and fleet. *Stratególos* was the only elective office that could be held more than twice, the only one that could be held in successive years. The pre-eminent position of Pericles is usually viewed as being greatly furthered by his nearly continuous holding of the office from the year 443 to his death.

3. Archidamus, King of Sparta and leader of the invasion, and Pericles were linked as *xénoi*, that is, by a relationship of friendship and mutual obligation between themselves and their families. The translation of *xénos* as "guest-friend" is conventional in English, there being no exact equivalent.

4. Part of Spartan strategy at the beginning of the war was to invade Attica annually, destroy standing crops, damage farms, and so attempt to weaken Athenian economy and morale.

5. Among the preliminary diplomatic moves of the war had been a Spartan demand that the Athenians expel from Athens the descendants of the Alkmeonid family, whose most prominent member at the time was Pericles himself. The basis of the demand was that an ancestor of the family had, about 630 B.C., incurred religious pollution by killing supplicants during an attempted military coup. Thucydides says [1.127] that the true reason for the ultimatum was not religious feeling but the desire to make Pericles unpopular in Athens.

6. The *talent* was the largest unit of accounting, being equivalent to 6,000 drachmas. As head of the Empire, Athens collected from its members contributions in the form of ships or money. Accumulated funds, controlled by Athens, were stored on the Acropolis.

7. The Propylaea were the monumental ramp, gates, and picture gallery designed by the architect Mnesi-

cles and erected to provide, on the west side of the Acropolis, an impressive entrance to the main sacred areas above.

8. Potidaia was a town on the peninsula of Pallene in the northern Aegean. It was an ally of Athens, but under Spartan and Corinthian influence revolted against Athens in 432. The Athenians laid siege to Potidaia as punishment but it did not surrender until the winter of 430.

9. Offerings or memorials in the form of sculptures, vessels, and other objects, frequently made from precious metals, had accumulated in large numbers on the Acropolis. They were the property of the divinity to whom they were dedicated, forming part of the temple treasuries.

10. Various valuable objects seized or captured from the defeated Persians in 480 and 479 were kept as trophies on the Acropolis. These included such items as the golden throne of Xerxes and the luxurious fittings of the tents of the Persian general Mardonius.

11. The statue of Athena housed in the Parthenon was a masterpiece of the sculptor Phidias. It was constructed of gold and ivory; the parts made of gold were her clothing, armor, and weapons. These were fastened to the armatures in such a way that they could be removed in case of need and the gold would, in effect, be taken on loan from the divine treasury.

12. Hoplites: the infantry of the Greek armies at this time.

13. Metics were residents of Athens who did not have Athenian citizenship. They were numerous and formed a large part of the city's permanent population.

14. The system of walls around Athens and its seaports

had been developed in stages over several generations. The city's walls were joined by the Long
Walls of those around the ports (the Piraeus and
Munychia) that lay to the southwest about three
miles from the city. A third harbor, at Phaleron,
was also linked to Athens by a wall. The linear
unit here is the stadium; the total of 148 stadia of
wall is equivalent to about 26,000 meters.

15.   Trireme: the standard Greek warship. A galley with
three tiers of oars on each side.

Comments on Summary of a Speech

Thucydides includes in his *History*, besides the
three Periclean speeches which he offers in direct quota-
tion, this summary of a speech delivered before the
Assembly at the beginning of the first campaign of the
war.

The lofty, hortatory tone of the other speeches is, of
course, absent from this summary. It is clear from the last
sentence, however, that the actual speech certainly con-
tained such passages. Thucydides' decision to summarize
this particular oration illustrates his selective approach
to the use of speeches. Some modern historians might, in
fact, prefer to have the complete original text of this
speech dealing, as it does, with many financial and military details, than to have the renowned Funeral Speech
that follows. But Thucydides' purposes are not those of
the modern historian; here he summarizes rapidly, in the
Funeral Speech he gives a fuller version.

The delivery of the speech occurs at the beginning
of the war. As the first invasion of Athenian territory is
imminent, Pericles realizes that he must ensure the citizens' full understanding of his relationship to Archidamus and that he must announce his intentions about

his country property. His care in avoiding suspicion of
friendly treatment from the enemy may appear to be
curious. It illustrates, however, his incorruptibility and
the frankness with which he approached the Athenians—
qualities which must have added to his stature as a
leader. Perhaps related to the issue of not appearing to
be receiving favors from the enemy leader is the casual
mention of the statue of Athena. Pericles' opponents had
tried to undermine his position by attempting to prose-
cute Phidias, the statue's designer and Pericles' friend,
on the grounds of theft of some of the gold used in the
statue. Yet, here Pericles lists that gold among the assets
of Athens, with no comment by Thucydides on Pericles'
relationship to the sculptor.

The survey of the economic and military resources
of Athens at this point, when hostilities began, is also
carefully planned, especially since Thucydides gives as a
reason for the writing of his *History* that opposing sides
were at that time at the height of their powers. The
inventory of financial details illustrates Pericles' insistence in the First Speech that money is necessary for the
winning of a war. The precision and the apparent com-
pleteness of the figures help to substantiate his policy.
They also anticipate his claim in the Funeral Speech that
public life in Athens is open: he has no fear of producing
in public a complete financial review of the city's resources. Thus Pericles once again persuades by means of
his frankness and logic. This enumeration of Athens'
impressive fiscal resources must have been astounding to
other Greek cities; it also must have greatly reassured the
Athenian citizenry. (It has often been noted, however,
that nowhere in the *History* does Thucydides include a
comparable survey of the financial resources of other cities, Sparta or Corinth, for example.) The unique position of Athens in the Greek world is broadly hinted at
in terms of wealth, even before Pericles in his Funeral

Speech stresses Athens' uniqueness in many other re-
spects.

From a rhetorical point of view the summary
presents material that Thucydides undoubtedly considered important, either for its own sake or as an illustra-
tion of Pericles' way of persuading the Assembly. The
questions of Pericles' property and the dry inventory of
resources would not, perhaps, form the basis of an oration sufficiently elevated in tone to be included in the
History. But the other speeches, read against the information presented here, gain greatly in depth.

THE FUNERAL SPEECH

◆⧖◆

(34) That same winter, the Athenians commemorated, at public expense, the funeral of those soldiers who were the first to die in the war. In doing so, they were following the custom of their fathers.[1] The ceremony is as follows: They construct a tent in which, two days before the ceremony, they lay out the bones[2] of the fallen soldiers. During that time, individuals make whatever offering they wish to their own dead. On the day of the funeral procession, coffins made of cypress wood are carried on wagons, one coffin for each tribe,[3] with the bones of each warrior from that tribe inside. One empty bier is decorated and included in the procession. This represents the missing dead, those whose bodies could not be recovered. Any citizen or foreign resident who wishes to may join the procession. The women who are relatives of the dead are also present and make their lamentations at the burial. The coffins are buried in the public cemetery,[4] which is located in the most beautiful area just outside the city walls. Except for those who die at Marathon they always bury soldiers who die in war in this cemetery. (Those who fell at Marathon[5] were buried on the battlefield because the Athenians thought that their bravery was exceptional.) When the remains

have been laid in the earth, a man, chosen by the citizens for his intellectual gifts and his public esteem, delivers an appropriate speech in praise of the dead. After the eulogy, all depart. During the entire war, when the occasion arose, the Athenians followed this ancient custom at their funerals.

Pericles, the son of Xanthippos, was chosen to speak over these first war dead. When the moment arrived, he came forward from the tomb, and standing on a high platform so that his voice might reach as far as possible in the throng, spoke as follows:

(35) "Many of those who have spoken here in the past have praised the custom of delivering this eulogy. They felt it was right to make such a speech honoring the soldiers who have fallen in war. As for me, our performance of this burial suffices to show respect for the glories of these men, who have shown their bravery by their performance in battle. You have just seen the deep respect demonstrated in this burial solemnized by the state. Our belief in the valor of these men should not depend on whether one man's oratory is good or bad. The burial ceremony itself is preferable to the risk of putting the acts of bravery of numerous men into the custody of a single orator who might speak well or badly. It is also not easy to find the right words when the occasion and subject of the speech make it difficult to persuade the listeners that the words are true. One listener who loved the dead and knows what the events on the battlefield were, might very well believe that the amount of praise fell short of what he wanted to hear. Another listener, however, not so informed, may think that the orator is overpraising the dead because that listener feels envy for the dead whenever he hears about exploits that go beyond his own capacities. Praise of other people is tolerable only insofar as the hearer believes he, too, has the ability to do the things he is hearing about; but whatever goes beyond that excites envy and disbelief.

However, since our forefathers set up this custom and approved of this practice, it is my duty to abide by custom and to obey the law, and to do my best to meet the wishes and expectations of every one of you.

(36) "I shall speak first of our ancestors. It is only right and proper on such an occasion to pay them the honor of evoking their memory. Our forefathers always lived in this land,[6] they handed it down from generation to generation to our own day, and, by their bravery, they kept it free. They certainly deserve our praise, and still more so do our own fathers deserve it. For what our fathers inherited from their fathers, they added to the empire we have now, and it was not without blood and toil that they handed it down to us, the generation now living. And we ourselves, assembled here, who are now for the most part still in the prime of life,[7] have increased the power of the empire in many ways and have made Athens the most self-reliant of all cities, whether in peace or in war. I have no desire to make a long speech on subjects familiar to you all. I shall then say nothing about the military exploits by which we acquired our various possessions, nor about the battles in which we, or our fathers, repulsed our enemies, Greek or barbarians. I shall first explain how we have arrived at our present greatness, what our political institutions are, and what are our characteristics as a people.[8] Then I shall proceed to the praise of these dead. For I think that such a speech is not inappropriate on the present occasion and that it is a good opportunity for this whole assembly of citizens and foreigners to listen to it.

(37) "Our form of government does not imitate the laws of our neighboring states. On the contrary, we are rather a model to others. Our form of government is called a democracy because its administration is in the hands, not of a few, but of the whole people. In the settling of private disputes, everyone is equal before the law. Election to public office is made on the basis of

ability, not on the basis of membership to a particular
class. No man is kept out of public office by the obscurity
of his social standing because of his poverty, as long as he
wishes to be of service to the state. And not only in our
public life are we free and open, but a sense of freedom
also regulates our day-to-day life with each other. We do
not flare up in anger at our neighbor if he does what he
likes. And we do not show the kind of silent disapproval
that causes pain in others, even though it is not a direct
accusation. In our private affairs, then, we are tolerant
and avoid giving offense. But in public affairs, we take
great care not to break laws because of the deep respect
we have for them. We give obedience to the men who
hold public office from year to year. And we pay special
regard to those laws that are for the protection of the
oppressed[9] and to all the unwritten laws that we know
bring disgrace upon the transgressor when they are
broken.[10]

(38) "Let me add another point. We have had the
good sense to provide for our spirits more opportunities
for relaxation from hard work than other people.
Throughout the year, there are dramatic and athletic
contests and religious festivals. In our homes we find
beauty and good taste, and the delight we find every day
in these things drives away our cares. And because of the
greatness of our city, all kinds of imports flow in to us
from all over the world. It is just as natural for us to
enjoy the good products of other nations as it is to enjoy
the things that we produce ourselves.

(39) "The way we live differs in another respect
from that of our enemies. Our city is open to all the
world. We have never had aliens' laws[11] to exclude anyone from finding out or seeing anything here, nor any
secrets of the city that an enemy might find out about
and use to his advantage. For our security, we rely not on
defensive arrangements or secrecy but on the courage
that springs from our souls, when we are called to action.

As for education, the enemy subjects their children from their earliest boyhood to the most laborious training in manly courage. We, with our unrestricted way of life, are just as ready to face the same dangers as they are. And here is the proof. The Spartans never invade Attica using only their own troops, but they bring along all their allies. But when we attack a nearby city, we usually win by ourselves even though we fight on enemy soil against men who defend their own homes. No enemy, in fact, has ever engaged our total military power because our practice is constantly to attend to the needs of our navy, as well as to send our troops on many land excursions. Yet, if our enemies engage one division of our forces and defeat it, they boast that they have beaten our entire army, and if they are defeated they say that they lost to our whole army. So it is not painful discipline that makes us go out to meet danger, but our easy confidence. Our natural bravery springs from our way of life, not from the compulsion of laws. Also we do not spend our time anticipating the sufferings that are still in the future, and when the test is upon us, we show ourselves no less brave than those who are continually preparing themselves for battle. Athens deserves to be admired for these qualities and for others as well.

(40) "Our love for beauty does not make us extravagant, and our love of things of the mind does not make us soft. We regard wealth as something to be properly used and not as something to boast about. Nobody need be ashamed to admit poverty, but it is shameful not to do one's best to escape from poverty. Our concern for our private affairs is balanced by our involvement with the affairs of the city. Even people who are mostly occupied with their own business are extremely well informed on political matters. We do not simply regard a man who does not participate in the city's life as one who just minds his own business, but as one who is good for nothing. We all join in debate about the affairs of the city, as

they deserve, or at least we participate in the decisions. We do not think that these discussions impede action. We do believe that what is damaging is to go into action in a crucial situation before the people have been fully instructed in debate.

"The strongest are those who understand with perfect clarity what is terrible in life and what is sweet and then go out undeterred to confront danger.

"But he who owes us something is likely to be listless in his friendship, knowing that when he repays the kindness, it will count not as a favor bestowed but as a debt repaid.

"Again, in nobility of spirit, we differ from most others in the way we conduct ourselves toward other peoples. We make friendships[12] not by receiving kindness from others but by conferring it on them. Helping others makes us a more trustworthy friend, because we then act so as not to lose the good will that our help created. A city that makes its friendships by accepting help is not so trustworthy. Its conduct toward other peoples is going to be governed not by good will, but merely by its grudging sense of obligation.[2] We alone do kindness to others, not because we stop to calculate whether this will be to our advantage, but in the spirit of liberality, which motivates us.

(41) "In short, I assert that the city of Athens, taken all together, is a model for all of Greece, and that each Athenian, as far as I can see, is more self-reliant as an individual and behaves with exceptional versatility and grace in the most varied forms of activity.

"And that this is no mere boast inspired by the occasion but actual truth, is attested by the very power of our city, a power that we have acquired as the result of these qualities. Athens alone, when put to the test, is superior even to her reputation. It is Athens alone that makes an attacking enemy not feel ashamed by being defeated by her. Nor does she cause her subjects to feel unhappy because they are ruled by unworthy people. Because of these mighty proofs of our power and because of the universal acknowledgment of our power, we are an object of wonder to men today and so we shall be to future ages. We shall not need the praises of Homer[13] nor anyone else's whose applause may delight us for the moment but whose presentation of the facts will fall short of what is really true. Our adventurous spirit has gained us entry into every sea and every land, and everywhere we left behind us memorials of suffering inflicted on our enemies and good done to our friends.

"Such then is the city for which these men nobly fought and died deeming it their duty not to lose. It is only fitting that every one of us who survived those men, will want, for Athens, to continue the toil.

(42) "And it is for this reason that I have dwelt at such length about our city, for I wanted to show that for us there is more at stake than there is for others who do not enjoy our privileges. And at the same time, I wanted to provide clear proof of the reality on which I based my praise.

"The most important words have now been spoken. I have sung the praises of our city. The gallantry and the splendid achievements of these men and of others like them have adorned it. There are not many Greek cities whose praise could balance that of Athens without having the reality mock the words.

"Such a death as these men died seems to prove the bravery they showed, how it only begins to reveal itself at first, but how, in the final test, it stands there quite unshakeable. Some of the men may have had their shortcomings, but what we must remember above all is the valor with which they faced the enemy and fought in defense of their homeland. They have blotted out evil with good and rendered more service to the state than they ever did harm in their private lives.

"None of these men became cowardly in battle

thinking that he would like to survive to enjoy his wealth. None of them persuaded himself to avoid facing danger hoping that he might escape poverty and become wealthy. More than these concerns, they desired to punish the enemy, regarding such a hazard the most glorious of all. And they accepted it, determined to strike down the foe and to forget about everything else. Whether success or failure, both still uncertain, they left that in the hands of hope. But in action, when the reality of battle was before them, they put their trust in themselves. They preferred to stand their ground and to die, rather than to yield and save their lives. They fled, indeed, from the shameful word of dishonor, and with life and limb they stood the brunt of battle, and in the climactic moment of their lives they finished their task, not in the grip of fear, but at the height of glory.

(43) "These men conducted themselves in a manner worthy of our city. We who have survived may hope to have a safer life, but we must resolve to show the enemy a spirit that is no less courageous. And you must estimate the advantages of such a spirit not just by a speaker's words—he could make a long story of what you yourselves know as well as he—but by all the advantages to be gained by warding off the foe. You should rather fix your gaze every day on the greatness of Athens and become her devoted patriots. And when the vision of her greatness has inspired you, then reflect that all this has been achieved by men of daring, men who knew their duty, and in the hour of conflict were moved by a high sense of honor, men who would be ashamed to do poorly in their work. If they ever failed in an enterprise, they were resolved that, at any rate, their city should not find herself deserted by their valor but instead that they would give the best offering it was in their power to give. They gave their lives for that common good and for themselves they won praises that will not grow old, the

most distinguished of sepulchres—not the sepulchres in which they now lie, but where their glory is laid down in everlasting remembrance, to be recalled whenever crucial moments of decision and action arise in the future. When men are so renowned, the whole world becomes their gravesite. And it is not only the inscriptions on their graves in their own land that commemorates them, but also in foreign lands there abides in every breast their unwritten memorial, planted in hearts rather than graven on stone.

"It is for you to make these men your models. Be convinced that to be happy means to be free and that to be free means to be brave. Therefore do not take lightly the perils of war. For it is not the wretched and unfortunate who have the most reason to fear death, for they have little hope for better days, but rather those who fear a complete reversal in their lives during times of hardship and crisis. For a man of self-esteem, humiliation because of cowardice is more painful than death, when it comes unperceived while you maintain your self-confidence and shared hope.

(44) "For these reasons I shall not commiserate with the parents of the dead who are present here but rather comfort them. They well know that they grew up in a world of many vicissitudes. It is good fortune for these men to have ended their lives in glory and for you to lament them. Their lives were balanced when death and happiness came to them simultaneously. I know that it is difficult to convince you of this, for you are going to be reminded of them often when you see the happiness of the living, the happiness that you once shared. Real grief does not come from being deprived of good things that one never experienced, but from the loss of something one is used to. You must find strength in the hope for other children, if you are still at an age to have offspring. These new children will not let you brood over those

who are no more. And they will be a help to the city, both by not leaving places empty and by assuring her security. For it is impossible for a man to offer fair and impartial counsel about our affairs, if he has no children whose lives are not risked. But as for you who have passed your prime, I would ask you to count as gain the greater part of your life in which you have been happy, and remember that what remains of it will not be long. And let your hearts be lifted up at the thought of the fair fame of these your sons. Love of honor is the only feeling that does not grow old. And the last pleasure when one is weak with age is not, as some say, making money, but having the respect of our fellow men.

(45) "As for those of you here who are sons or brothers of the dead, I can see a great conflict awaits you. Everyone will naturally praise those who are no more. And even if you were to attain surpassing heroism, it will be a hard thing for you to be judged their equal or even having come near their virtue. For there is jealousy of the living because of rivalry. But once a man is no longer in one's way, the honors he receives are sincere and no longer curtailed by jealousy.

(46) "I should also speak of womanly virtues thinking of those who henceforth will be widows. I will sum up all in a brief admonition. Not to fall below the standard that nature has set for you will be your greatest glory, and great, also, is that of a woman who is least talked about among men, be it in praise or in blame.

"I have now spoken, as the law demanded, and said what I had to say. Those we have buried here have been properly honored, and for the future, their children will be supported at the public expense until they come of age. This is the prize and the wreath the city offers, both to the dead and the bereaved, for the ordeals they have faced. For where the prizes offered for virtue are greatest, there you will also find the best citizens.

"And now, having made due lament for your dead, you may depart."

Notes on the Funeral Speech

1. It was the practice among most Greeks to bury their dead on the battlefield where they fell. Thucydides underscores the exceptional nature of this Athenian practice.

2. Presumably the dead would be cremated either on the battlefield or in Athens and their bones preserved until the time of the annual ceremony.

3. Athenian citizens were enlisted for various administrative duties among the ten tribes.

4. Thucydides does not name the cemetery, which is now known as the Keremeikos, located just outside the Dipylon Gate near the Agora.

5. The Athenian funeral mound at Marathon, known as the Soros, still exists. We know that the Athenian dead were also buried on the battlefield of Plataea, so Thucydides' statement about Marathon's exclusive burials is incorrect. Gomme in vol. II, pp. 94–101 offers a thorough discussion of this inconsistency.

6. Athenians, like many other ancient communities, solved the riddle of their most remote origins by believing that their ancestors were autochthonos, that is, born from the land in which they lived.

7. "Pericles' own generation (he was now not much over 60), say of 465 to 440 B.C." (Gomme.)

8. The exposition of background extends from section 37 to 41, while the eulogy extends from 42 to 43.

9. Any person who so wished could initiate an action on behalf of a wronged person. Under older practice, only the wronged party or a relative could bring such an action.

10. These were all traditions and customary prohibitions which people obeyed as if they had been laws, although they were not written down. Punishment for breaking such laws was the resultant inner feeling of shame, and of community disapproval for having transgressed an almost religious standard of normal and decent behavior.

11. Sparta restricted associations between citizens and foreigners and, in general, did not tolerate outsiders.

12. The friendships referred to here are not primarily private relationships, but diplomatic or treaty relationships, to which Pericles applies the terminology of individual psychology.

13. Pericles presumably refers to the renown attached to Mycenae, Troy, and other such prehistoric sites by the Homeric poems. The identity of the "glib contemporary writers" is not known and is disputed. Presumably Pericles means something like pretentious chronicle writers.

14. Greeks often took a pessimistic view of old age and various writers dealt with its deprivations; the reference here may be to the poet Simonides.

Comments on the Funeral Speech*

For the historian, Pericles' Funeral Speech is a valuable statement about Athenian democracy in the fifth

---

* No full literary and historical analysis of the speech has been published in English. The section on the speech in Edmunds' *Chance and Intelligence in Thucydides* (pp. 44–70 offers an excellent analysis of many passages, but it was not intended as a complete commentary. I have found the following useful: J. T. Kakridis, *Der Thukydideische Epitaphios: ein stilistischer Kommentar* (Munich, 1961); H. Flashar, *Der Epitaphios des Perikles: seine Funktion im Geschichtswerk des Thukydides* (Heidelberg, 1969); G. P. Landmann, "Das Lob Athens in der Grabrede des Perikles," in *Museum Helveticum*, vol. 34 (1974), pp. 65–95.

century. It is, besides, a masterly and quite original handling of the ideas that can be expressed on the occasion of a public military funeral. Some commentators have asserted that it is an intensely personal statement by Pericles of his own interpretation of Athens' place in history and his justification of the Athenian empire and its spirit. Transcending its occasion, the speech poignantly points to a possible relationship between the individual, his fellow citizens, and his native land and its civilization.

Thucydides records [34.1] that the public burial of soldiers killed during each year's military campaigns was an annual ceremony at Athens. This information would interest non-Athenian readers of the *History*. The differences between Athens and other Greek cities, which are a basic theme of the speech, begin with this fact, for it is implied that no other Greek city had this custom. Thucydides does not assign a date to the beginning of the custom, but it probably began at the time of the Persian wars.

Since an oration was part of the ceremony, it follows that there had been a considerable number of preceding orations and that others were delivered as the war went on and as circumstances permitted. Yet Pericles' oration is the only one of its kind that Thucydides quotes. It is probably right to conclude that his was included in the *History* from among all possible ones because Pericles was chosen by the people to speak on the basis of his outstanding oratorical ability, and because Thucydides was especially concerned that his readers should grasp what Pericles attempted to convey to the Athenian people on this occasion.

The *epitaphios*, as this kind of oration was called in Greek, consisted of a number of recognized topics: praise of the dead, praise of the ancestors, praise of the city, consolation of the families of the dead. The success of the

orator on each occasion would be measured by how well
he renewed, combined, and varied traditional topics.
Pericles touches upon them all, but the extent and in-
tricacy of his departures from a routine treatment of the
standard topics are very striking.

In the opening lines (35.1) Pericles hints at the
complex manner in which he will handle the topics of a
funeral speech. What men have said in the past is the
opposite of what, he believes, should be said in the
present. Pericles mentions the customary opening words
("It is a good tradition to give this speech") only to
reject its theme. His own thought is paradoxical as are
many other points in his oration: the best speech, it appears, would be no speech at all. The action of the ceremony, he believes, adequately corresponds to the action
of the soldiers. But he will go on to speak nevertheless,
out of respect for the tradition surrounding the ceremony.

The related topic of the inadequacy of the orator for
the occasion is developed in some detail. Relying on his
own abilities as an orator, Pericles says that if he speaks
well, the achievements of the soldiers will have been
equaled. The intellectual performance of the orator is
potentially equivalent to the military performance of the
soldiers. As the argument develops, we discover that the
reason for this equivalence is that the orator and the
soldier understand the nature of their city, the orator
when he proves its greatness and expounds on its qualities, the soldier when, at the most crucial moment of
battle, rather than refuse to die he decides to protect his
city.

The peculiar difficulty of the orator is to find words,
a generic difficulty that is compounded by the occasion of
this particular speech, the *epitaphios*. It demands praise
of the soldiers who died, which, however, is valueless if
his statements are not believed to be true. The difficulty

is to strike a balance between two types of listeners. One type appears to be familiar both with what the men did and with speeches given at previous public burials. Pericles expresses no great concern about this class of listeners, but the other type commands more attention. This type is unfamiliar with eulogies and will have the impulse to reject what they hear because they cannot credit it. Pericles does not see this negative instinct as one based on mere skepticism, but he analyzes it in terms of personal envy and lack of imagination. The passage is important, for it anticipates Pericles' insistence later in the speech that there are proofs of the extraordinary claims he makes about Athens. (In routine patriotic orations both the orator and the audience share a cliché-ridden concept of the greatness of their country. Pericles attacks the Athenians' reluctance to recognize the greatness of Athens throughout the speech, but the attack is indirect.) The passsage is also, in rhetorical terms, a proof of the truth of what is going to be said in the eulogy, because the claim to truth is strengthened by the advance warning that it will be difficult to believe. This "proof" is neither unfamiliar ("You won't believe what I'm going to say, but . . .") nor subtle. But it does involve the audience in the orator's claims about the greatness of Athens. If what he says in praise of Athenian soldiers arouses envious disbelief among some Athenians, this fault does not lie with the soldiers, nor with the orator, but with the civilians who cannot measure up in generosity and imagination to the undoubted achievements of the soldiers. The passage, which seems to be a pedantic or even an antagonistic passage, actually lays down a step in the argument of the speech, an argument that will emerge completely when Pericles calls for the citizens to become lovers of Athens in the same way as did the soldiers who died.

In the next section [36.1] he praises the ancestors,

but only briefly. The mythical period of Athenian history, in particular the reign of Theseus, is omitted, although we know from other speeches that this was almost obligatory. Praise of Athens in the time of Theseus would have involved mentioning the early political organization of Attica, and perhaps even the earliest stages of human civilization in the region, when Athena, for example, presented Athens with the olive tree and when Demeter at Eleusis taught Athenians agriculture. But Pericles confines himself to recent and non-mythological phases of history. He speaks of three generations: the ancestors, the fathers, and his own generation. The division breaks down into the generation of the Persian wars, the generation that founded the empire, and the generation responsible for developing the financial and military power of Athens to its highest peak. Pericles concentrates on contemporary Athens as *the* center of strength and power, a city that need not look to the very distant past for legitimation. Yet Pericles explicitly rejects understanding Athens' recent development primarily in terms of battles and military exploits. One feels that Pericles here is making a marked departure from the usual treatment of the topic. He finds the strength of Athens elsewhere, in its customs, the character of its people, and its form of government.

To praise Athens, then, is to praise the Athenian people rather than Athenian history. This agrees with what Pericles says elsewhere: that the city would, if necessary, be abandoned during wartime, but that the city would survive if the citizen body were kept intact (First Speech, section 143). It is not difficult to see this as an echo of the Themistoclean strategy of abandoning Athens in the crisis of 480–479 B.C., when the citizens were removed *en masse* before the Persians arrived in Athens.

The character of the Athenians is implicitly contrasted with that of the Spartans. Athenians are open, not secretive; they find time for enjoyment; they welcome and enjoy foreign goods; they are easy-going among themselves; their educational system is relaxed and successful; they handle wealth intelligently; the poor are not discouraged; citizens take an interest in government and those who do not are criticized. The contrast with Sparta is not made explicit at all points, but may be filled out fairly easily. Sparta was a closed society, suspicious of foreigners and of foreign goods; Sparta educated its youth from boyhood onward in a strict militaristic fashion, which included informing as a means of control; Spartan society was dour in tone; laws limited the accumulation of wealth; the individual was not encouraged to take part in public life. Pericles argues not only that Athens and Sparta are different, but goes beyond that to assert that Athenians are the equals of Spartans with regard to bravery in battle and obedience to laws and to those in authority. The crucial question is, which of these two contrasting societies proves itself to be the more powerful? The paradox, of which Pericles offers proof, is that Athens, although it is not geared to military success, has more power than Sparta and *a fortiori* than any other Greek city. Athens, an open and attractive society, rises superior in sheer strength to the closed militaristic society of Sparta.

Pericles' brief and allusive description (37.1) of the government of Athens has caused much controversy. He obviously did not need to list the magistracies and offices, or to analyze the day-to-day workings of the government with which all his listeners were familiar. Pericles emphasizes the name of the Athenian form of government, "democracy," because the object of government is not the interests or prestige of only a few individuals or of a small group. He wants to make clear a different meaning of "democracy"—the power of the majority to dominate

the state—is not why that name is given to their government. His definition of democracy is rather negative. He
lists other characteristics. The laws apply equally to all
men. Participation in office-holding is open to all regard-
less of wealth or poverty. The man who has something to
contribute is not prevented by the majority from making
his contribution. Democracy is therefore a balance. It
does not work to the advantage of a small group, but
neither does it exclude the selection of leaders who are
from among the most capable.

Everything is done *eleutherōs,* in a "spirit of freedom" (37.2). This word applies to the atmosphere of
Athenian life rather than to any stated political or civil
right. Yet with this word Pericles aims to describe the
most important condition under which Athenians act.
Laws are obeyed not because of the dread that a slave
might feel before a master, but from a spontaneous feeling of respect for the laws and magistrates. (Later Pericles will analyze the courage of Athenian soldiers in
analogous terms.) Hence the laws that provide recourse
for the wronged and the unwritten laws of decent behavior are singled out as being especially carefully
obeyed. Such laws obviously involve finer feelings, such
as good will and charity, than laws against ordinary
crime. Hence the rather unexpected description of the
daily atmosphere of life among the citizens. Pericles says
that the "spirit of freedom" prevents Athenians from
being self-appointed censors of each other's normal life
within the law.

The physical and cultural delights of the city are
dealt with briefly (38.1). Some critics regretted that Pericles had not made specific references to architecture,
playwrights, artists, and musicians. But Pericles implies
all these things without telling his audience what they
already know. (A principle he adheres to throughout
the speech: see 36.4 and 43.1.) Furthermore, his tone is

statesmanlike; his concern is to speak in analytical generalizations rather than in specifics. (We never hear, for example, of how many soldiers were buried or in which battles they fell.) So in this passage Pericles describes the delight in being an Athenian, without giving specific examples of the source of those pleasures.

Since the mention of pleasure in Athenian life might be considered trivial, Pericles turns to the military courage of that city's soldiers (39.2). To understand this passage best, it would be well to remember that Athenian armies, like those of other Greek states, were basically citizen-armies and that for Athens the war against Sparta required a total effort on the part of the population. A significant portion of the people would be affected by the war, since there was no professional military class. Also, the resident population of the city was increased by refugees from the country, all living virtually under siege for several months of the year. Hence Pericles is anxious to show that the government, the atmosphere of the city, and the Athenian educational practice are responsible for the city's military accomplishments.

Athens, then, presents a remarkable balance. Its care to provide a place for beauty and enjoyment in life does not prevent it from living a life of practical and effective action. Throughout the speech runs the idea that many believe wealth, and the ease and enjoyment to which wealth gives access, robs men of courage and initiative. Pericles denies this truism, saying that wealth leads Athens in general into action and that the thought of achieving or enjoying wealth does not prevent its soldiers from dying courageously on the battlefield. Similarly, Pericles challenges the notion that discussion and acting with confidence are mutually exclusive, saying that the citizens in general do not lose courage when they indulge their right to debate in the assembly and that the dead

soldiers were braver than others because they faced
death, not with a kind of brute bravery, but with
resoluteness based on knowledge of the worst.

Pericles' praise of Athens is therefore praise of all
Athenians for willingly participating in the life and
spirit of the city. This idea, I believe, comes closest in the
whole speech to defining the distinctive quality of
Athenian democracy. Pericles saw (and eulogized) the
importance of the participation of all Athenians. It was
not government by all the people (a kind of mon-
strosity), nor government for the benefit of all the people
(an impossibility), but government in which all the people took an active and informed part. Pericles widens the
scope of his praise to say that discussion in the Assembly
sets the Athenians apart from all other Greeks, not just
from Spartans. Indeed, the practice of debate before
going into action leads to greater resoluteness in Athens
than in other cities, which is a characteristically paradoxical (and perhaps Periclean) reversal of what most
Greeks would have regarded as the true relation between
debate and action.

The section on friendship (40.4–5) is intended to
illustrate further the Athenians' sense of freedom. Pericles claims for them a spontaneous, generous outlook.
His argument is based on the curious question: Who is a
better friend, one who gives help, or one who receives
help? Pericles' answer agrees with the views held by others exploring the concept of friendship that the person
who gives help makes the better friend. The reason is
that the person who gives help will then be the object of
gratitude of the person who received help. Who, in that
case, would be more likely to terminate the friendship?
The person who *owes* gratitude is more likely to do so
than the person to whom it is owed. Therefore the person who helped another is a more trustworthy friend.
The argument is not about personal friendships, but

about the relationship of Athens to other cities. They should not be afraid to receive the help of Athens, for by so doing they will be securing a good ally.

Pericles' praise of Athens is now complete (41.1). He sums it up in the famous phrase about Athens being the "model for the rest of Greece." (*Paideusis*, translated here as "model," literally reads "means of educating.") Pericles' intention becomes clear when he carefully balances his assertion about the city as a whole with what he believes to be true about individual Athenians. The individual Athenian has in a degree superior to all other Greeks the benefit of a good education. Pericles is aware of how extravagant his claim sounds, but he says that he can prove what appears to be exaggeration to be the truth. Athens' strength is proved by a paradox: enemies do not feel frustrated when Athens defeats them. Therefore Athens has achieved the enviable position of being an object of wonder. And for ever after, instead of traditional words of praise by poets, enduring monuments in near and far places will bear witness to Athens' greatness.

Pericles states that his praise of Athens is neither false nor irrelevant. If Athens were not the kind of city that he describes, the soldiers would not have died for her. The war is about the preservation of Athenian characteristics. The fallen soldiers' courage was not uniform or constant, but it proved itself at the right moment, and because the individual performed one act of courage for the common good, any previous shortcomings were erased. The benefit of the state transcends the impulse to blame the weakness of the individual. The actual moment of decision on the battlefield is brought before the audience's mind (42.4), but not as description of the battle, but as a psychological vignette. Pericles tells his listeners how the soldiers remained true to the values of Athens by rejecting the chance to save their lives and unhesitatingly resisted the lure of the pursuit of a life of wealth and rather faced the enemy and death.

The quality of morale in the civilian survivors should be comparable to the quality of bravery in the dead. Pericles scoffs at mere self-defense. Any orator, of course, can explain how self-defense is a desirable thing. But the civilians will only act like soldiers if they are motivated not by calculation but by a deep emotional motive, by love, in fact, and love will arise only from active contemplation of the power of Athens. Pericles then draws the link again between the greatness of the city and the men who preserved that greatness. Their reward is eternal fame, which transcends space and time. If it exists in the minds of Athenian generations to come, then it will be forever active, a sign of greatness. The fate of the dead soldiers is thus in the hands of the civilians, or more specifically in the hands of Pericles' audience. If they do not become lovers of Athens, then they will not realize its greatness, and if they do not grasp its greatness, then they will not remember the men who helped preserve its greatness and the soldiers will have died in vain.

The praise of the soldiers is now complete and Pericles turns to the surviving citizens. The speech proceeds to the consolation of the living parents (44.1). Pericles advances another paradox: no consolation is necessary for these parents because they are actually fortunate to be able to mourn bravely for their children who died bravely for Athens. This seemingly insensitive argument is softened by the admission that feelings of grief are unavoidable. Pericles exhorts the mourners to take solace in the thought that at least those young enough to have more children will be parents of future citizens and defenders of Athens. His argument contains the subtle hint that those who have children are better, more concerned, advisers in the city's affairs.

Addressing those listeners who may be too old to have children anymore, Pericles rejects the notion that the chief delight of old age is the accumulation of wealth. Rather, he suggests satisfaction should be derived from being parents of soldiers who valiantly died defending Athens.

Pericles then turns to the children and brothers of the fallen. Their lives are to be interpreted in terms of the dead fathers and brothers. As they achieved undying fame, the competition will be cruel, for Pericles assumes that these male survivors will want to emulate their dead relatives. It is a minor but characteristic point in the structure of the argument. Pericles has so elevated the dead that he can hardly suggest that it will be easy or even possible to surpass them. So he notes the difficulty of the conflict and the unfairness of competing against dead opponents who are safe from criticism. The passage, reminiscent of discussion of athletic competitions in its use of metaphor, suggests the enormous pressures that developed in the Greek agonistic view of life.

His last words are to the widows. He admonishes them to maintain their womanly virtues. It is a moot question whether this short passage can be taken as evidence, as some have done, of the status of women in classical Greek. Pericles promises the widows that the children of the fallen soldiers will be supported at public expense. He calls this arrangement a victory crown. The children, as wards of the state, will be guaranteed the education that will make them into representatives of the Athens for which their fathers died, and for which they too will come to know how to die instinctively.

THE THIRD SPEECH

After the second invasion by the Spartans, the Athenians began to change their minds about their policy. This was the second time that their territory was being ravished and the plague[1] was continuing to accompany the war. They began to hold Pericles responsible, because he had persuaded them to go to war and because he seemed to be the one who had entangled them in these disasters. They were strongly inclined to make an armistice with the Spartans. They actually sent some negotiators to Sparta, but the mission did not accomplish anything. They seemed to have become stuck with a policy that brought them no results, and so they attacked Pericles.

He realized that the short-term results of their policy were causing them anxiety, and their behavior was precisely what he had anticipated. Since he was still general, he called a meeting of the Assembly. He wanted to increase their confidence in themselves, as well as to use persuasion to change their anger at their policy into a mood of more self-control and less fearfulness.

He appeared before them and made this speech:

"I was expecting that your anger against me would

come out into the open, because I know the reasons for it. Therefore, I have called this Assembly in order to remind you of some past events and to present the arguments that are required in the face of your unreasonable anger and your loss of morale caused by the recent turn of events.

"I believe that the citizens are better served when the whole city is prospering than when the city is doing well only from the point of view of some of its citizens, but as a whole is going downhill. A man may be doing very well, but if his country is ruined, he will be ruined as well. If, on the other hand, the city is prospering while he is not doing so well as an individual, he is nevertheless protected. Therefore, since the state can support its citizens in their misfortune, but no one person by himself can save it from its misfortunes, it is surely the duty of all citizens to rally to the state's defense.

"You should not be acting the way you are. You are so confounded with your own afflictions that you ignore the common safety. You now blame me because I urged and persuaded you to go to war, and you blame yourselves for voting for it.

"If you are angry with me, it is with one who is, I believe, second to none in formulating policy and making that policy clear in debate, one who moreover loves this city and who is above being influenced by money. A man who has that ability but not the one clearly to express it, might as well have no idea at all on that matter. A man who has both these gifts, but lacks love for his country, cannot speak for his own people as he should. And even if he is also patriotic, but unable to resist a bribe, then the whole state could be purchased for whatever price he would take.

"If you then believed that I had the abilities that I mentioned, to a slightly higher degree than had others, and if you then took my advice and went to war, it seems unreasonable for me now to be accused of having done wrong.

"If one can live undisturbed, and has the choice between war and peace, it is utter folly to go to war. But if one is forced to choose between submission and immediate slavery, and taking the risk of war to preserve his independence, then the man who avoids risk is to blame, not the one who puts up resistance. As for me, I am the same as I have always been, and I have not changed. It is you who are changing because you took my advice to go to war when you were still not harmed, but now that you are suffering harm, you repent of your action. The argument I used to persuade you then does not appear to be correct now, but only because you are weak in your determination. It is a policy that entails suffering, and you already know what this suffering is. It grips the feelings of each one of you, while the proof of the ultimate benefits that you will gain is still far away.

"Now that a sudden reversal of events has befallen us, you are too dejected to persevere in your resolve. For the spirit is cowed by that which is sudden and unexpected and altogether unpredictable. And just this has happened to you with the plague added to it all. Yet, you are citizens of a great city and have been raised in a way of life that matches its greatness. You must therefore be willing to face even the greatest calamities and be resolved to keep unimpaired the glory that is yours. We all detest people who arrogantly claim a reputation that they don't deserve; but we equally have contempt for those who, through faintheartedness, fail to live up to the reputation they have already won. Cease, then, to grieve for your own particular afflictions, and join in a common effort for the safety of us all.

"And if you think that our suffering during this war may become greater and greater, and we may still not have a happy result, let those arguments suffice that I have often used on other occasions to show you the groundlessness of your fears. Now to those arguments I will add another one, which concerns the sheer size of the empire. This argument, it seems to me, you have never thoroughly grasped in all its significance, nor have I mentioned it in my former speeches. It is an argument that I would not use even at this time, because it is a somewhat boastful claim, had I not seen that you are unreasonably discouraged.

"You think perhaps that your empire extends only over your allies. But I will demonstrate to you that you control, by yourselves, one of the two great divisions of the visible elements, land and sea. That is, you have absolute mastery over the part in your power and over as much more of it as you may wish. With your navy, such as it is today, there is no power on earth, neither the King of Persia nor any other people, who will stand in your way when you set sail. The power that you control on the sea is something entirely different from the benefits that you derive from your houses and cultivated lands, which you think are too great assets to risk losing. You may think that their loss would be a great privation. But you should make light of them, regarding them as no more valuable to you than a flower garden or some rich man's trinket, if you compare them with your navy, the real source of your power. And you should recognize that liberty preserved by your own efforts will easily recover for us what we have lost. But if we submit to others, we shall lose what we now have.

"You must not show yourself inferior to our forefathers who did not receive an empire from others but won it by their own toil and sweat. They preserved it so that they could hand it down to us. It is more of a disgrace to have taken away from you what you have already got then to fail in the attempt to get something. You should go forward to meet the enemy, not only with

self-confidence, but with a sense of superiority. Even a
coward can feel self-confident if he has a run of luck. But
the feeling of superiority comes only to those who, like
us, have real reason to be assured of their superiority
over their adversary. And when the chances on both sides
are equal, it is discernment that fortifies a feeling of
superiority that enables us to look down at our adversary. It puts its trust not in hope, which is the prop of
the desperate, but in reason supported by facts, from
which a more secure anticipation of the future may be
obtained.

"It is your proper task to support the position of
eminence that Athens has gained from its empire. You
all take pride in this eminence. But you cannot share in
its glories, if you decline to shoulder the burdens of our
empire. You should not think either that the struggle is
only one over the question of freedom or slavery. Involved also is the loss of our empire and the dangers
created by the hatred we have incurred in administering
it.

"Nor is it any longer possible for you to give up this
empire, if indeed any of you, either out of panic or love
of peace, acts as if this were a noble thing to do. The
empire you hold is a tyranny.[2] It may have been wrong
to take it, but it is extraordinarily dangerous to give it
up. If men who talk about abdication persuade others,
they will destroy the city almost immediately, even if
they go off to live by themselves under their own laws.
For those who don't take an active part in the work of
the city will survive only if they are supported by people
who are willing to take action. They are useless in a city
that controls an empire, but by submitting as slaves, they
would be safe in a city controlled by others.

"Do not be led astray by citizens such as these, nor
should you be angry with me, for you yourselves voted
for the war the same way as I did. Certainly the enemy

has invaded our country and has done what he was expected to do, as soon as we were not willing to yield to
him. The plague from which we are suffering also fell
upon us beyond what we could foresee. But of all the
things we have suffered, that is the only one that tran-
scended our foresight. I know, that because of the
plague, the displeasure with me is greater than it would
be otherwise. But that isn't right, unless you are also
going to put down to my credit every piece of unexpected good fortune that comes your way.

"Men must endure with resignation what the gods
send, but with fortitude, the hardships that come from
the enemy. Such attitudes have been ingrained in the
character of this city and now especially we should not
let them go. Remember also: Athens has the greatest
name in all the world, because she has never yielded to
adversity, but has lavished more life and labor in warfare
than any other state, thus winning the greatest power
that ever existed down to our time, a power that will be
remembered forever by posterity, even if we should ever
be forced to yield, because all that is born will decay. Yet
it will be remembered that we, of all Hellenes, ruled
over more Hellenes than anyone else and that we stood
firm in the greatest wars against them, whether they were
united or alone, and that we lived in a city that was the
richest in everything and the greatest.

"All this may be disparaged by those who take no
part in matters of the polis, but those who, like us, prefer
an active life, will imitate us; and if they do not achieve
what we have achieved, they will envy us.

"To be unpopular and hated for a time is the lot of
all those who think it is worthwhile to rule over others.
But if there is a great goal to pursue, this burden of odium
must be accepted, and it is a wise decision to accept it.
For hatred does not last long, but the splendor of the
present is the glory of the future preserved forever in the

memory of man. It is then for you to safeguard that future glory and do nothing now that is ignoble. And attain both these goals by devoted efforts.

"Do not send heralds to the Spartans. Do not betray to them any sign of being bowed down by your present afflictions. Those who are least disquieted when they face calamity but vigorously react to it, they, whether they are cities or individuals, are the strongest of all."

Notes on the Third Speech

1. A severe plague broke out in Athens in the winter of 431 causing many deaths and much demoralization. It infected Thucydides, who recovered, and Pericles, who died.

2. Tyranny was control of the government by a single man or family supported by military force. As a form of civic government it had died out in classical Greece, but several episodes of tyranny in earlier Athenian history were well remembered and referred to frequently.

Comments on the Third Speech

The selection and position of Pericles' Third Speech in the *History* are carefully chosen. Thucydides follows it with an elaborate assessment of Pericles' abilities and of his policies and their fate. This assessment includes the information that Pericles died of the plague two years and six months after the outbreak of the war. The Third Speech therefore represents (in Thucydides) Pericles' last public defense of himself and his policies.

The setting of the speech, clearly explained by Thucydides, recalls the setting of the First Speech. At

that time, an embassy from the Spartans came to persuade the Athenians not to begin war. This led Pericles
to address a meeting of the Assembly. In this Third
Speech, an embassy from Athens to Sparta might, under
pressure of military losses and the plague, succeed in
arranging a truce. Thucydides states very plainly that
this speech is an attempt at persuasion, an effort to
change the mood of all the citizens.

Pericles acknowledges the anger that the citizens feel
toward him personally. He even says that he anticipated
the anger would come, thereby demonstrating in himself
the kind of foreknowledge and intelligence that he says
the city itself should have. His argument is to make himself the spokesman of the city. His opponents and critics
are merely expressing their individual and shortsighted
resentments and frustrations. In asserting that concern
for the city's prosperity should take precedence over the
feelings of individuals, Pericles is making a point that
recalls his analysis of the weaknesses of the Spartan alliance in the First Speech. Sparta's inability to merge the
private concerns of her allies toward a common purpose
results in weakness and indecision. The need for leadership and unity is critical for states at war.

Against the changeability and the easy discourage-
ment of the Assembly, Pericles sets his own constancy
and self-confidence. This, however, is not expressed in
terms of personal pride, but in terms of the public activities of the statesman. The leader must have a policy,
must be able to expound that policy, and persuade others to adopt it. Above all he must be *philopolis*, a "lover
of the city." Pericles admits that other leaders may have
one of, or a combination of, these abilities in various
degrees, but he possesses all of them at once and to a
greater degree than others. The unspoken part of this
argument is that, at the beginning of the war, Pericles
did have a policy, he did persuade the Assembly to adopt

it, and he did show, in the Funeral Speech (and perhaps in his being selected to deliver that eulogy), that he had a unique understanding of the quality of Athenian life. There he took the lead among "friends of the city" by urging other citizens to turn themselves into "lovers of the city" and by showing them how and why it should be done.

The thrust of these arguments is not that Pericles wants to deny or usurp the authority of the Assembly in a crisis. Rather, he wants to clarify the implications of its actions to the Assembly and to urge that it be consistent, patient, and farsighted.

The speech thus repeats some of the arguments of the first two speeches. A new element, as Pericles points out, is his analysis of the Athenian empire. The most notorious phrase in this analysis is his assertion that the Athenians hold the empire "like a tyranny." Pericles does not conceal the element of power used in the establishment of the empire and in its maintenance. But he does not state that the empire is in fact or should be a tyranny. His subject is neither the acquisition of the empire nor the quality of justice in its maintenance. He is talking only about the possible relinquishing of the empire, which he knows would be forced upon Athens by an accommodation at this point with Sparta. It is the relinquishing of the empire that he compares with the relinquishing of a tyranny. He is attempting to persuade the Assembly that the advantages of sea power are decisive, that these advantages are linked to the empire, that the empire would begin to break up should Athens make any accommodation to Sparta, and that the break-up of the empire would be extremely dangerous for Athens. No friend of the city would advocate a retreat from the imperial position. The argument is thus a call to the Assembly to take a long view of the consequences of precipitate action, to accept that the benefits of their empire are bound up with responsibility and that this responsibility must be maintained with intelligence and courage.

Pericles' brief analysis [62.4] of the relationships between luck and hope, intelligence and courage, is most remarkable. He rejects the habit of seeing human endeavors as a series of unforeseeable and unavoidable events. Those who put their trust in luck and hope are abandoning their own courage and intelligence, which are, in combination, characteristic of the Athenian traits he had described in the Funeral Speech. Here he acknowledges that the plague has been devastating Athens and demoralizing the people. Yet the plague was (and this is a crucial point) unforeseeable. Pericles argues that the plague should not change at a stroke the very character of the Athenians, for their character is based on their knowledge of the best and the worst. If they begin to hope that fortuitous events will come their way and that bad accidents (like the plague) will befall their enemies, then the distinction between the Athenian and Spartan character will vanish, for luck is wholly neutral. With no such distinction the war, by implication, is not worth fighting.

The call of Pericles then is for responsibility, steadiness, and true courage based on intelligence and foresight. What is to be the Athenians' reward? The speech contains an unemphatic but unmistakable note of traditional Greek pessimism: "disintegration attacks everything men create." This generation of Athenians, the fabric of the city itself, and the empire, will not last forever. Pericles acknowledges that they have no hope of creating or maintaining an everlasting civilization. Why fight then? The argument for reaching an accommodation with Sparta might appear to be strong if the effort required to hold out against Sparta will not lead to the permanent establishment of the pre-eminence of Athens.

Pericles' argument is that the display of courage against Sparta will result in what he calls "contemporary brilliance and future glory." Athenian civilization will certainly disappear, but the desire in future generations to recapture it and to emulate it will never disappear—not if the Assembly sticks resolutely to Periclean policies. The argument is breathtaking, yet clearly based on the traditional Greek view of fame and good reputation, those imperishable rewards of skill and bravery in Homeric battle or of hard training and strength in the athletic contests celebrated by Pindar. Momentary success may be converted into immortal fame. The Athenians, in their Assembly and under Pericles' leadership, may make a crucial contempoary decision that will have the effect of overcoming the destructive effects of time.

BIBLIOGRAPHY

Note: Among complete translations of Thucydides' *History,* that of Rex Warner (Penguin Books 1954, revised edition 1972) is the best. The *Oxford Classical Dictionary* (second edition 1970) is useful for fuller references to persons, places, and institutions. The following bibliography is selective and confined to works, mostly recent, in English.

Adcock, F. E. *Thucydides and His History.* Cambridge: Cambridge University Press, 1963.
    Adcock deals with most of the important Thucydidean questions and offers a theory about the publication of the *History* after the death of Thucydides.
Bradeen, D. W., "The Popularity of the Athenian Empire," *Historia,* vol. 9 (1960), pp. 257–269.
    Bradeen attacks the arguments of de Ste. Croix—the Athenian Empire was not popular; Thucydides' picture is essentially correct.
Cawkwell, G., "Thucydides' Judgment of Periclean Strategy," *Yale Classical Studies,* vol. 24 (1975), pp. 53–70.
    Cawkwell defends the historical accuracy of the policies outlined in Pericles' First Speech.
de Romilly, J. *Thucydides and Athenian Imperialism,* trans. P. Thody. Oxford: Basil Blackwell, 1963.
    De Romilly, among the best recent students of Thucydi-

des, attempts to throw light on the problems of the *History*'s composition by studying Thucydides' attitude toward the Athenian Empire; the chapter on Pericles (pp. 110–155) offers a very useful discussion of his speeches.

de Ste. Croix, G. E. M., "The Character of the Athenian Empire," *Historia*, vol. 3 (1954), pp. 1–41.

The essay presents the case that Thucydides' picture of the unpopularity of the Athenian Empire is distorted and that Athens was unpopular only with conservative minorities in the subject cities.

——. *The Origins of the Peloponnesian War*. London: Duckworth, 1972.

The Introduction (pp. 1–34) attacks the speeches of Thucydides in an original way.

Dover, K. J. *Thucydides*. Oxford: Clarendon Press, 1973. [*Greece & Rome*: New Surveys in the Classics, no. 7.]

Dover's brief account is a thoughtful and learned introduction to Thucydides and the scholarly research that he has inspired.

Edmunds, L. *Chance and Intelligence in Thucydides*. Cambridge: Harvard University Press, 1975.

Edmunds studies *gnome* and *tyche*, "intelligence" and "chance," and related words, especially in the speeches of Pericles, with close analysis of many passages from them.

Finley, J. H. *Thucydides*. Cambridge: Harvard University Press, 1942.

This, in spite of its date, is perhaps the best general study of Thucydides in English.

Gomme, A. W., "The Speeches of Thucydides," in *Essays in Greek History and Literature*, Oxford: Basil Blackwell, 1937, pp. 156–189.

Gomme vigorously attacks those who assume that the speeches are free inventions of Thucydides and presents both evidence and arguments to corroborate their authenticity.

——. *A Historical Commentary on Thucydides*, Vol. I and II. Oxford: Oxford University Press, 1950; 1956.

Gomme's is the standard historical commentary on Thucydides; his volumes I and II cover books I, II, and III of the *History*.

Jones, A. H. M. *Athenian Democracy*. Oxford: Basil Black-well, 1957.

This collection of articles provides good discussions of Athenian society in terms of its political, economic, and military organization.

Kagan, D., "The Speeches in Thucydides and the Mytilene Debate," *Yale Classical Studies*, vol. 24 (1975), pp. 71–94.

Kagan restates and extends Gomme's views of the historical accuracy of the speeches.

———. *The Outbreak of the Peloponnesian War*. Ithaca and London: Cornell University Press, 1969.

———. *The Archidamian War*. Ithaca and London: Cornell University Press, 1974.

Kagan's volumes present a full critical narrative of the background of the Peloponnesian War.

McGregor, M. F., "The Politics of the Historian Thucydides," *Phoenix*, vol. 10 (1956), pp. 93–102.

McGregor describes the anti-democratic family background of Thucydides and offers an explanation of his approval of Periclean democracy.

Meiggs, R. *The Athenian Empire*. Oxford: Clarendon Press, 1972.

This is a detailed study of the Empire's history and the historical problems associated with it.

Parry, A., "Thucydides' Historical Perspectives," *Yale Classical Studies*, vol. 22 (1972), pp. 47–61.

Parry analyses the personal and tragic qualities of the *History*, with an attempt to reconstruct Thucydides' historical "system" and Pericles' unique place in it.

Stadter, P. A. (ed.). *The Speeches in Thucydides: A Collection of Original Studies with a Bibliography*. Chapel Hill: The University of North Carolina Press, 1972.

This is a useful collection of lectures on various problems connected with the speeches; it includes the best available bibliography of the speeches.

Walcot, P., "The Funeral Speech, A Study of Values," *Greece & Rome*, vol. 20 (1973), pp. 111–21.

Walcot discusses especially the section on widows (45.2), which he places in the context of traditional Mediterranean social values.

Westlake, H. D. *Individuals in Thucydides*. Cambridge: Cambridge University Press, 1968.

    This study of Thucydides' interest in individual leaders and of his techniques of describing and evaluating them also attempts to throw light on the questions of dating and composition; Pericles and his speeches are dealt with on pp. 23–42.

Woodhead, A. G. *Thucydides on the Nature of Power*. Cambridge: Harvard University Press, 1970. [Martin Classical Lectures, vol. 24.]

    Woodhead pursues the thesis that Thucydides' central concern was power in its many manifestations and illustrates his discussions with abundant historical and philosophical citations.